Uncovering G

Book one

Sandra Brack and Bob Dixon
Gateshead Local History Society

Uncovering Gateshead – Book one
Five heritage walks around Gateshead

Do you sometimes walk down a street and think 'I have never noticed that before' or 'I wonder what that was used for?' This book takes a look at a variety of buildings and street art located around Gateshead which have a historic interest, an unusual purpose, or we just think are interesting.

In this first book of three, the authors take you on five walks one around the Town Centre, two around Bensham, one around Saltwell and one around Shipcote.

We hope this book will be enjoyed by everyone whether you are a walker, interested in local history or want to find out more about Gateshead.

Acknowledgements

The authors would like to thank Gateshead Library, Tyne and Wear Archives, Bede Methodist Circuit Archives, Jon Bratton, Shirley Brown, Andrew Clark, Tony Diston, DP Supplies, Trevor Ermel, Fullis Wholesale Ltd, Meg Gilley, Moira Inness, R. Johnston, Anthea Lang, David Owen and St Chad's Community Project. Also thanks to all those unnamed people who kindly gave us their support.

Bibliography

History of Gateshead – F.W.D. Manders 1974
Gateshead's Grand Houses – Sandra Brack 2012
Saltwell Park – Anthea Lang 2013
Gateshead Remembered – Anthea Lang 2014
Gateshead From Old Photographs – Sandra Brack, Margaret Hall
and Anthea Lang 2015
Gateshead's Grand Houses Revisited – Sandra Brack, Bob Dixon,
Margaret Hall and Helen Ward 2016
Ordnance Survey maps
Ward's trade directories
www.gracesguide.co.uk/McKenzie_and_Holland
www.twsitelines.info
www.workhouses.org.uk/Gateshead

Copyright © Gateshead Local History Society 2018
First published in 2018 by
Summerhill Books PO Box 1210, Newcastle upon Tyne NE99 4AH
www.summerhillbooks.co.uk   email: summerhillbooks@yahoo.co.uk
ISBN: 978-1-911385-21-9

Our first walk is around the **Town Centre** and is approximately 2.5 miles.

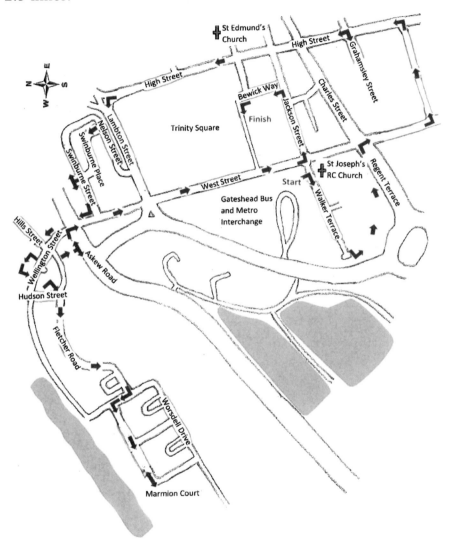

We start our walk at Gateshead bus and metro interchange, where you can see the 2004 art work 'Opening Line' by Danny Lane. The sculpture made from steel and glass is over 90 metres long and rises to a height of over 5 metres. From here note St Joseph's Church on the corner of Walker Terrace, built in 1859 with contributions from 'the faithful Catholics of the parish of Gateshead'.

We now walk up the beautiful Georgian street Walker Terrace built c. 1847, at the top note the stone street sign shown right. Turn left where you will see this street sign.

It is a reminder that Prince Consort Road continues down to Askew Road, and above the sign view a lovely bay window.

To the right of the columned doorway you will see this large brass plaque listing the one time occupiers of this building.

Now turn around and look over the dual carriageway where you will see the old Day Industrial School on Windmill Hills which opened in 1880. In later years it became a residential home and has been closed for many years. It is now in the process of renovation.

We now take the little path around the building and at the corner you will see this unusual chamfered brick feature.

Cross over the car park and along the little footpath then turn left onto Regent Terrace, which was built c. 1852 and occupied by shipbrokers, gentlemen, accountants and coal owners, and faced onto gardens. From here over the roundabout you can see the Gateshead Bowling Green Club founded in 1865. We now turn left and walk down Regent Terrace, on the corner is a single storey building. This was originally the gatekeeper's house for the street. Note the Lambton Lodge stone sign.

At the traffic lights cross towards Gateshead Civic Centre, which was opened in January 1987 by Neil Kinnock.

Now cross over High West Street, turn right and continue past the Gloucester public house then turn left down Ann Street. Here we turn left onto the High Street, a little way along on your left is an old bricked up doorway with 'Camerons Building 1897' inscribed on the stone lintel (*shown right*).

The photograph below shows a horse and cart outside Camerons Buildings in 1929. The shops are Ferris's advertising their 1st Anniversary Sale and Hadrian selling tea; then to the left is Harris's cycles and through the archway is the Empire Garage; these were later demolished for the Odeon Cinema.

Continue to the corner of Grahamsley Street and High Street, then facing the William IV public house you will see a blue plaque to the 19th century song writer Geordie Ridley best known for 'Blaydon Races'.

Glance over the road where you can see an old tiled shop frontage which was once Dietz pork shop. The green and cream tiled front was added in the 1930s.

Then walk towards Charles Street passing Curley's public house on your left, named after Will Curley the professional boxer and later publican.

Crossing over Charles Street we arrive at the Metropole public house, note the tiled flooring depicting the word SCALA. This old doorway was once the entrance to the Scala cinema. It originally opened as the Metropole Theatre on 28 September 1896. It was converted into a cinema in 1919 and re-named the Scala. The cinema closed in 1956 and became a warehouse. If you glance up at the side of the building you can see the theatrical characters which are a reminder of the buildings former usage.

Look at the row of shops across the road and note the stylish frontage of the building on the left. Built in 1933 for Arthur Doggart at a cost of £30,000, it sold everything but food and was one of 17 Doggarts department stores in the north east. The photograph left shows the store before it closed in 1970. Observe the metal panels interspersing the floors which feature a 'D' monogram, with the faience pilasters between them continuing the theme.

Cross over Jackson Street to the corner, note the lovely green and white mosaic floor of the shop entrance. We now cross over High Street to St Edmund's and Holy Trinity Church. Located against the right hand wall you can see the old entrance to Gateshead House which stood behind the chapel. This gateway was moved to the forecourt of St Edmund's Chapel when Holy Trinity was built.

If open, walk inside where you will see the mask of the Blessed John Ingram, a catholic priest who was executed for his beliefs at a gallows outside this church on Friday 26 July 1594, age 29 years. Also in the church you will see the churchwardens' chair of 1666 from St Mary's Church.

We now look back over the road to the building next to the lane (*shown below*). Admire its decorative embossed panels which create vertical separation between the large metal window frames of the first and second floor frontage. This three storey commercial premises was built as one shop for Montague Burton (Burtons) by their in-house architect, Harry Wilson.

 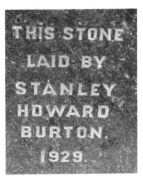

Right: The foundation stone on High Street.

Carry on down the High Street to the Grey Nags Head public house at its junction with Leonards Court. This was named after James Leonard whose market garden once stood on this site. There were 15 deaths in this street during the third cholera epidemic of 1853.

Cross over the High Street passing the new shopping complex and take the pedestrian crossing over Lambton/Nelson Streets. Bear left then turn immediately right and follow the road curving to the left down Swinburne Place.

First we come to the old Police house on the left. Then straight ahead is the former Fire and Police Station building (*shown right*) which still has the old cells underneath.

Continue into Swinburne Street, cross over the road and with the car park behind you admire one of Gateshead's finest streets. These buildings included a post office, building society, bank and the old library. As you walk to the corner of Swinburne Street note the clock tower of the old Town Hall by the architect John Johnstone which was built in 1868.

We now turn right down West Street to the traffic lights at Askew Road. Cross over and go under the railway arch into Hills Street. On your right is the Station East public house. If open why not call in and see the splendour of the newly discovered Robert Stephenson railway arch.

From here cross over Hills Street toward the Maccoy Fountain which was relocated here on 3 December 2015. The fountain is in memory of Sir John Maccoy's wife Rebecca who died due to injuries sustained in a car accident in 1914.

Maccoy was mayor of Gateshead on eight occasions and is the only mayor of Gateshead to be knighted.

Glance over to the opposite side of the street and you will see the boarded up area where Gateshead Bus Station once stood. The photograph right shows the station in 1980.

This site was once known as 'the Butts' probably where mandatory archery practice took place during the reign of Henry VIII, and later the site of the Eighton Moor and Team Colliery Depot.

We now walk around to the right under the railway bridge into Half Moon Lane, which was originally called Bailey Chare.

Carry on under the bridge and look to your right where you can see a bricked up archway. This was one of the entrances to the old Gateshead Railway Station which opened on 18 June 1844. The station was renamed Gateshead East Station on 1 December 1868 when Gateshead West station opened.

You can see Gateshead Station entrance to the far right of the drawing below.

Now glance up to the top right hand corner of the wall where you can see the old street sign Railway Passage (*shown right*) – what a wonderful name.

Behind you on Half Moon Lane stands the Central Bar, historically referred to as 'The Coffin' due to its unusual shape. The pub was used in the film 'Women in Love' starring Oliver Reed, Alan Bates and Glenda Jackson and more recently the final episode of 'George Gently' starring Martin Shaw.

Turn right and walk along Mirk Lane once an old cattle route leading to the river. Greenes Tannery stood on the left side near the railway arches, and to the right side was a paper works. Follow the path around to your left passing new steps leading to the Hilton Hotel.

Now turn left and go under the railway arch onto Wellington Street, then look at the first archway on your right. This used to be a second entrance to Gateshead East Station.

The photograph above was taken from inside the station which closed on 23 November 1981.

Cross over Wellington Street where you can see two small archways. The first quaint entrance with a smart stone surround has two metal gates which take you into a cobbled lane and may have been an old entrance to buildings behind. If open you can walk through the lane and come out at the other small archway again with metal gates which is part of the Railway club. The building between these gates is now apartments called Worsdell House named after the railway engineer of the same name. At the back of the building stood the High Level Bridge Inn.

We now carry on along Wellington Street towards the High Level Bridge. Turn left onto Hudson Street and walk up the right hand side and turn up the car ramp to the top. This was at one time the entrance to Gateshead West Railway Station which was opened on 1 December 1868 and closed on 1 November 1965.

Walk back down the ramp onto Hudson Street and turn right under the railway arch by Robert Stephenson. You are now in the modern development of Ochre Yard, which is on the site of

the old Greenesfield Railway yards. Walk along Fletcher Road and at the mini-roundabout turn right. Continue along Fletcher Road then turn left and walk along the road. Near the end, on your right hand side, you will come across the building (*shown left*) that was once the boiler shed, now being developed.

Carry along the footpath behind Marmion Court to the open paved area near Midlothian Court. If you look over the wall you can see the Metro Bridge from a unique angle.

Retrace your steps back to Hudson Street and walk along the back of the Railway club, to Half Moon Lane. The building on the corner was once the Commercial Hotel.

Now turn right and follow the narrow footpath, originally part of Half Moon Lane, which takes you under the railway line and brings you out on Askew Road.

Here we turn left and walk along Askew Road, parallel with the railway line. Not far along you will come across an old metal pillar in the wall, a remnant of our railway history.

The words on the pillar are McKenzie & Holland Worcester England No 9 signal lever frame. The company made levers, points, signals and signal boxes.

Continue along Askew Road to Wellington Street and cross the road at the traffic lights then up West Street to the front of the old Town Hall building, which opened in February 1870 and was where council meetings were held until the opening of the new Civic Centre on Regent Street in 1987. Since then it has been a temporary home of the Royal Northern Sinfonia Orchestra during the construction of The Sage Gateshead, later the Tyneside Cinema and again part of The Sage Gateshead. In 2017 the building and surrounding land was put up for sale and it is soon to have a new use.

Here also stands the gothic-style cast iron clock tower which was designed by Gillott and Johnson of Croydon. It is inscribed:

'Presented to the Borough of Gateshead by Walter Willson, Mayor 1892.'

The clock is painted black and gold and is a facsimile of 'Little Ben' at Victoria Station, London.

On the opposite side of West Street you can see the art work 'Acceleration' designed in 2005 by John Creed which acknowledges Gateshead's railway heritage.

Now walk to the corner with Nelson Street, note the plaque on the old Dispensary which provided health care in Gateshead from 1855 until 1946.

On the opposite side of Nelson Street between Tesco's and the former Lloyds bank building you can see the intriguing façade (*shown right*) of the rear entrance to the old post office on West Street.

From here continue up West Street and pass the old Lloyds Bank Chambers. The letters have been removed now but you can still see where they have been. Just next door we come to the old Post Office building. Here you can see two plaques, the top plaque made of metal commemorates the centenary of Thomas Bewick's death. The lower plaque made of granite identifies the actual site of his house.

In the wall to the right of the window note the hole and handle. This arched shaped foothold was used to assist the night watchman/policeman step up and take hold of the handle which would allow him to look through the window to check that the safe had not been broken into.

Next we come to the new Gateshead Trinity shopping complex where once stood the famous Shephards of Gateshead store, renowned for its money tokens (*above*) and sales jingle shown right. Emerson Shephard began his business in 1906 with a small shop in Swinburne Street, Gateshead, which later moved to the corner of West Street and Ellison Street in 1908. An extension was added to the headquarters in West Street and Ellison Street in 1934 which gave the store three floors. On the 18 January 1946 the store was destroyed by fire and Shephards moved to Kent House on Church Street while the store was rebuilt. The new store on West Street opened in 1951, and in 1980 Shephards store closed and re-opened as Shopping City. This store closed in 1986 and was later demolished.

Shephards of Gateshead
The biggest and the best store
Shephards of Gateshead
Have what you're looking for
There's so much to see
And the car park is free
Come shopping at Shephards
For the whole family

Over the road you can see the 1986 art statue 'Sports Day' by Mike Winstone, the first of many sculptures in Gateshead's Public Art Programme. Originally in colour this black sculpture shows a figure in a sack with a hare and tortoise.

Continue up West Street and turn left into Jackson Street. The photograph left shows the site of New Century House on the corner of Jackson Street or Chare as it was originally called.

Now head down Jackson Street passing the former Co-operative buildings, it is totally unique to have three Co-operative department stores on the same street. The first building is called New Century House and was built in 1964, the second built in 1925 in the Art Deco style; and the third opened in 1884, note the ornate frontage and the stone beehive, a co-operative symbol representing working together for the good of the whole. Next on your left you will see an old stone wall, built from stones from the windmill that formerly stood where New Century House is today. This would have been the rear wall of shops or warehouses at one time.

Note the slots in the wall and the small metal rings, it is thought an abattoir once stood near here.

From here turn left along Bewick Way and proceed into Trinity Square and turn left, just before the public conveniences, you can see a plaque on the wall about Gateshead Car Park. Now turn left into the public conveniences. Here in this rather unusual place you will find photographs and artwork of central Gateshead both past and present, and this is where our town centre walk ends, just a short distance from Gateshead Interchange.

Our second walk is around **Bensham** and is approximately 2.5 miles.

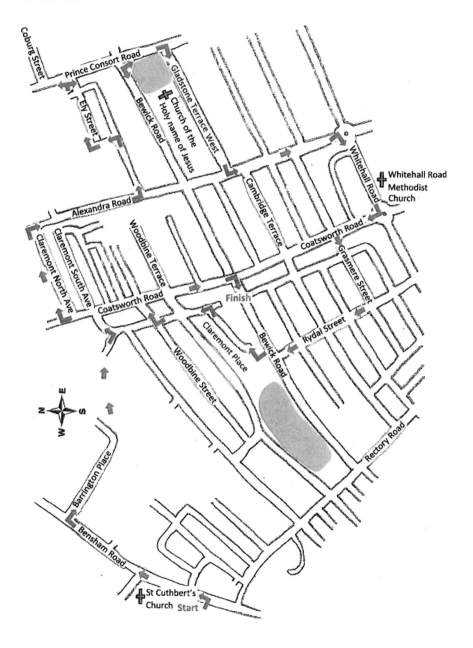

We start our first Bensham walk outside St Cuthbert's Church on Bensham Road, note the lovely surrounding wall on Second Street, next to the surgery.

The Foundation stone of St Cuthbert's was laid in July 1846 and the architect was John Dobson. The total cost was £2,000 which was raised through public subscription. If you are able to, why not take a walk around the churchyard.

On leaving the churchyard turn right and using the pedestrian crossing head towards Cotfield House, a detached Georgian house. It was built in 1806 for Thomas Thompson, a prosperous timber and raff merchant and local song writer, known most notably for the 'New Keel Row' and 'Canny Newcastle'.

Walk up the hill passing a terrace of houses with a private footpath. At the end of the terrace note the words Westview on the gate post.

Now have a close look at the lovely decorative stonework between the windows of the end house called Westview House, depicting a woman with a sleeping child, a scholar reading, sheep and flowers.

It is thought that Westview and the house next door were originally one house.

Doctor Alfred Cox once lived in Westview and on the wall you can see a blue plaque in his memory. Dr Cox whose practice was on the lower floor of Cotfield House, was influential in improving public health in the borough and helped found the Gateshead Queen Victoria Nursing Association and the Gateshead Medical Association. Spare a thought for the stone sheep supporting the porch since 1892.

Facing up hill, a little further on your right, are some new houses built on the site of the Five Wand Mill public house (*shown right*). This was named after Gateshead's only five wand windmill, later steam-driven, reputedly the best mill in Gateshead

which burnt down in 1858. One of the owners William Gibbon (1771-1846) is buried in St Mary's grave yard, now the home of St Mary's Heritage Centre opposite The Sage Gateshead.

From here walk a short distance up Bensham Road and turn right along Barrington Place, note the very old stone terrace on your left and the wall enclosing Barrington Villa at the far end. The Villa is a narrow L shaped house, one room deep, and appears to be two houses added together. It is thought that the building on the right is of older date which was a scullery with stairs to the upper floor, possibly servants' accommodation.

From here cut through the car park, passing to your right the Nursery House Working Men's Club, onto Coatsworth Road and turn left. Now cross over to Claremont North Avenue and walk along to the far end and on the left is an ornate brick wall featuring crafted indentations and coping stones. This wall partly surrounds a formerly detached Georgian house, now part of a terrace on Alexandra Road. Turn right and walk a little way along Alexandra Road. Here note the sign above the door Alexandra Hall. This building at one time hosted Evangelical services.

We now walk further south along Alexandra Road, passing two schools on either side of the road, then just before Bewick Road is a back lane. Walk along the lane, turn left then right into Ely Street and as you walk along the street observe the decorative panels above some of the upstairs windows.

Passing the Kingdom Hall (Jehovah's Witnesses) and Mosque (formerly the Christadelphian Church) we reach Prince Consort Road. Look across the road toward Denmark Street and see how the wall is cut away on the corner. This may have been a door to a shop which was a common feature of Bensham or perhaps designed to allow a horse and cart to negotiate the narrow streets.

The street to the left of Denmark Street is Coburg Street. In the 1971 film 'Get Carter', Michael Caine as Jack Carter stayed at a house in this street called 'The Las Vegas Hotel'.

Now turn right and walk along to Bewick Road. On the opposite side is a communal garden, look at the railings surrounding this park area and you will see some gates which would have led to individual private gardens (*shown right*).

Keeping the park to your right, turn into Gladstone Terrace West, note the lovely iron balustrade above the front portico of the first house on the left.

Carry on along the street, to your right is the Catholic Church of the Holy Name of Jesus (formerly Christ Church) and on your left is the National Spiritual church.

Now walk to the end of the street and turn left onto Alexandra Road and look at the ornate Dutch gable roof tops. Carry on to the cross roads and turn right down Whitehall Road to the

Methodist Church, which opened in 1896, and admire the tiled inlays in the brickwork.

We now walk to the right along Coatsworth Road, named after the Cotesworth family but misspelt, passing a distinctive curved wall and just a little further along is a lovely brick gable end which has inset brick work and a decorative stone lintel.

From here cross over Coatsworth Road at the zebra crossing and walk down Grasmere Street where we have an example of two different street signs (*shown below*). Observe the original sign of Grasmere Terrace carved in stone then at the other end of the street is the metalled sign, Grasmere Street, above which you can just about make out another old stone sign.

We now turn right and walk along Rydal Street towards Bewick Road, if you have time why not explore these Bensham streets which are full of interesting architectural details.

At Bewick Road turn left and cross over towards two stone gate pillars and cut through the right hand pathway into Claremont Place. Look at the lovely row of houses and compare with the old image left.

Claremont Place was built on land belonging to William Hymers, a local iron master. The terrace was built in three sections between 1819 and 1824, each house comprises of two storeys with a basement with dressed ashlar stonework to the front and random stone to the rear. Carry on through Claremont Place to Sedgewick Place a quaint little street tucked away behind the shops built in 1824.

On leaving Sedgewick Place cross towards the lane on your left and follow it through onto Woodbine Street. This was once the site of the Rectors Field/Union Workhouse which opened in July 1841 to accommodate 276 inmates

We now turn right onto Coatsworth Road where opposite we can see a mock Tudor building known variously as Hawks Dance Hall or as is shown in this advertisement Hawks' Assemblage.

HAWKS' ASSEMBLAGE

COATSWORTH ROAD, GATESHEAD.

GOOD FRIDAY.

DANCING 8—11.45.   ADMISSION 1/6.

EASTER MONDAY.

CARNIVAL DANCE

DANCING 8—11.45.   ADMISSION 2/.

To the right is the former Honeysuckle public house, rebuilt in the 1920s in an ornate and obtrusive late Edwardian style in red brick with stone dressings to its arched windows, a corner turret and accentuated gables.

Metropolitan Borough

Gateshead

WILLIAM BOOTH
(1829-1912)
Founder of the Salvation Army
and

CATHERINE BOOTH
(1829-1890)
Co-founder, the 'Army Mother',

lived here 1858-1861.
Catherine preached her first sermon
in Gateshead in 1860.

2005

Cross over Coatsworth Road and turn left up Woodbine Terrace, an eclectic mix of Georgian and Victorian houses. Near the top, on your left hand side is a blue plaque denoting the home of William and Catherine Booth from 1858 to 1861. William was a Methodist Minister during his time in Gateshead, he then resigned to pursue his evangelical beliefs and later founded the Salvation Army.

We now retrace our steps
back towards Coatsworth
Road, where you will
see an old stone wall on
your left which was the
original garden boundary
of

From here head left along
Coatsworth Road to the corner of
Bewick Road, here on your left is a
substantial stone gatepost.

Now turn right and cross over
Coatsworth Road to view the
imposing red brick building
formerly the Coatsworth Cinema
with a Neo-Byzantine tower, which
opened on 8 December 1913. It
closed as a cinema on 30 July 1960
and reopened as a Bingo Hall in
1962. The building is now owned
by the Jewish community.

Turn round to view the
two quaint little shops on
the opposite side of the
road, originally one
building and around
1935 to 1939 was
occupied by Mr R.E.
Hepple, an optician.

Return to Coatsworth
Road where our Bensham
walk ends. From here
you will be able to access
local bus services.

Our third walk is also around **Bensham** and is approximately 2 miles.

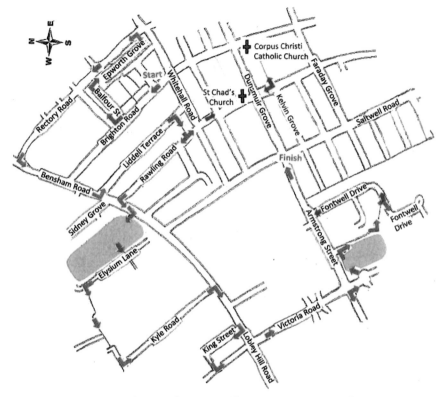

We start our second Bensham walk at the corner of Whitehall Road and Brighton Road, where you can see a large stone building. This was built as a Presbyterian Church, the foundation stone was laid by Alderman William Sutton JP of Newcastle on 1 March 1902.

This postcard shows Brighton Road with the Presbyterian Church on the right in the early 1900s.

Now walk along Brighton Road and turn up Balfour Street on your right. From here you can see the front of the old Vicarage with a large bay window facing west. Notice the bricked up gateway which may have been the main entrance at one time.

Continue right along the lane where you will see a door with two large stone pillar tops, presumably another entrance to the Vicarage.

Carry on along the lane, turn left and walk up Epworth Grove. Now turn right, a little further along you will see the first of two unusual street signs (*shown right*) with arrows directing you to Epworth Grove. From here turn left up the lane to find the second street sign.

We now turn left onto Rectory Road passing a row of houses with ornate plaster friezes between the bay windows.

Now walk to the end of Rectory Road passing the back of the old Vicarage.

Here on the stone wall to your left you will see a blue plaque to Emily Davies, co-founder of Girton College Cambridge and the daughter of the Rector of Gateshead.

From here walk down Bensham Road and along Liddell Terrace where we come across a lovely brick building built in 1899 for Colonel George Angus, a prominent Tyneside industrialist. Generally known as Angus Hall, it has distinctive regimental architecture betraying its origins as a Drill Hall.

The stone shield left shows 1st NTVA 1899 which stands for the 1st Newcastle upon Tyne Volunteer Artillery. This was a precursor to the Territorial Army.

Carry on along Liddell Terrace and turn right down the lane onto Rawling Road. The building in front of you was built in 1925 as a Primitive Methodist Church and has also been known as Trinity, Rawling Road and Whitehall Road West Methodist Church; and closed in 1994.

Cross over Whitehall Road and continue along Rawling Road to Westminster Street here you can see St Chad's Church, which was consecrated in 1903 with its magnificent octagonal tower. The church was designed by William Searle Hicks in the style of the Arts and Crafts movement, and built on land given by Lord Northbourne. The costs were born by Emily Easton.

Continue along Rawling Road to Kelvin Grove and on your right is the former Church of Christ Meeting Place. The old sign (*shown right*) is just visible under the church's new name.

Glance to the opposite side of Rawling Road and note the street sign on the corner house (*shown left*). The property used to be a bakery before being converted into a private house.

If you have time why not walk up
Kelvin Grove between the two schools to
the corner with Brighton Road, where
you will pass the ornate downpipe and
hopper of Corpus Christi Rectory.

Now turn left along Brighton Road to
Corpus Christi Church, opened in 1936.
This imposing edifice was built in red
brick on a reinforced concrete frame

with sandstone
dressing from the
local Springwell
Quarries. Observe
the grey/green
slated roof and
decorative drain
pipes.

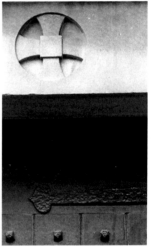

Also look for some
of the detailed stone
work as you walk
round the church
(*shown right*).

From here we
retrace our steps to
Whitehall Road, cross over and carry on along Rawling Road.
Near the end, on the left hand side, you will see a terrace
which unusually for Gateshead have basement flats.

At the end of the street we rejoin Bensham Road, cross over
and take time to look at Bensham Grove Community Centre, a
grade II listed building. This was owned in the early 19th
century by Joshua Watson, a cheesemonger and Quaker. His
son Joseph and later grandson Robert Spence Watson enlarged
the house which resulted in a strong Arts and Crafts theme.
On the death of the Spence Watsons, Bensham Grove became
an Educational Settlement doing much work during the
Depression in the 1930s. Bensham Grove to this day still
follows the principals of educating, promoting and improving
life in Bensham.

Continue down Bensham Road, originally part of Lobley Hill and Burnstones turnpike and note the prism-shaped sandstone milestone. The markings indicate G1 and W22, which stands for Gateshead 1 mile, Wolsingham 22 miles, and provides the traveller with a guide to how far they need to go or have travelled. A milestone is one of a series of numbered markers placed along a road or boundary at intervals of one mile or occasionally, parts of a mile.

Look across the road at the steel structure called 'Window' designed by Colin Rose in 1986. Just past the milestone go through the gate into the park which was originally part of Bensham Grove grounds. As you walk through you will come across this stone wall (*shown left*).

Then a little further round to the right what appears to be the partial remains of the garden boundary of Bensham Grove (*shown right*).

We now leave the park onto Elysium Lane, to your right is the gable end of Station Cottages. These were constructed for railway workers of Bensham Station which was in operation from 1868 until its closure in 1954.

Here we turn right and walk along Elysium Lane. Take the tunnel on your left under the first railway track and then the bridge over the second. From here you can see a lovely row of houses called Tynevale Terrace.

Close to Tynevale Terrace once stood Tynevale House, built in the late 1860s for George Dixon who lived there for more than twenty years. Dixon was a rope manufacturer of Dixon & Corbitt Ltd who later merged with R.S. Newall and Co. Both companies were established at the Teams in 1840, Dixon & Corbitt Ltd was on the east bank and R.S. Newall on the west bank, and had worked together for many years before amalgamation in 1887. One of their famous exploits concerned Cleopatra's Needle. Newall's supplied the wire rope and Dixon & Corbitt Ltd the steel caisson which were used to tow the obelisk to London from Egypt by sea. The amalgamated concern was taken over by the Willington Haggie firm and in 1959 became part of the British Ropes Group.

Facing Tynevale Terrace, follow the footpath to your left round onto Hazel Road, and turn left onto Kyle Road. As you walk along note the old stone wall and entrance on your right. Could this have been the old gateway to Roseville, once the residence of the architect Gibson Kyle who lived there for more than thirty years?

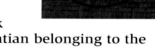

Carry on to the end of Kyle Road then turn down Lobley Hill Road and then right into King Street. At the far end of King Street you will come to the former Fentimans pop factory. Notice the sign in the brick wall of Fearless, the prize winning Alsatian belonging to the founder Thomas Fentimans.

Follow King Street around to your left onto Victoria Road and turn left back to Lobley Hill Road, where we cross at the lights.

Carry on along Victoria Road, walking through the Racecourse estate, note the horse's heads artwork on the grass area just after Aintree Gardens.

At the end of Victoria Road you come to Armstrong Street, turn right. A short distance down on your left you can see an old brick wall which at one time formed the boundary of the Gateshead Union Workhouse. In 1885 a competition was held for plans for the new workhouse and the joint winners were Messrs Newcombe and Knowles of Newcastle, and J.H. Morton of South Shields. The new workhouse was to accommodate 922 inmates, with a school for 300 children, at an estimated cost of £40,110.

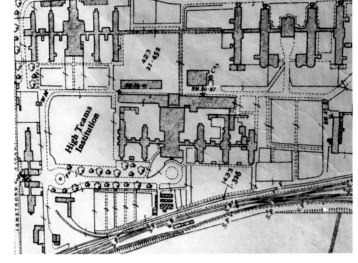

Shown right is a map of the workhouse site in 1939, after being renamed the High Teams Institution.

When I was very young in the 1920s my father had an allotment on what is now the north east corner of the Team Valley Trading Estate, known as Coronation Allotment.

You went down Armstrong Street and under the bridge that carried the main line trains from Newcastle to London. After the bridge you had the workhouse fields to your right, sometimes when these fields were not under cultivation I used to go there with my father and fly my kite.

On your left was the workhouse wall about 7 ft high stretching right down to the next railway line that took goods trains into the shunting yard at Greenesfield docks.

Half way down the wall was the main gate, when you looked through the large double gates you could see the fountain. At the west end the wall was slightly lower and we used to climb up to see the Piggeries, the smell was pretty rough!

Anonymous

Retrace your steps up Armstrong Street and turn right, this area along to Bensham Hospital was for many years part of the High Teams Workhouse. Here you can see the Penrose Fountain, named after Mr and Mrs Penrose the Master and Matron of the workhouse. The inscription on the base says – THIS FOUNTAIN WAS DESIGNED, SCULPTURED AND NAMED BY JOHN MOORE AN INMATE OF THIS INSTITUTION. Just below the top of the fountain there are two scrolls, one with the words – THE PENROSE FOUNTAIN and the other says ANNO DOMINI 1895.

Now glance over to the field where you can see the remains of an old stone wall, probably part of the workhouse building. From here walk up the narrow path on your left which brings you out at Wetherby Grove, turn right and walk along parallel to the field toward the houses until you reach a square grass area. Take the path to the left and walk through the archway onto Fontwell Drive. Opposite you can see corridors (*shown*

left) which would have provided both covered access to the hospital buildings and outdoor exercise with protection from the weather. Within the hospital grounds there still exists an original workhouse building which later became Bensham Hospital.

We now turn left and walk up and round Fontwell Drive, then right at Armstrong Street and under the railway arch. Continue to the top of Armstrong Street, on your right is a lovely old advertisement (*shown left*).

A few more steps and we are back onto Saltwell Road which is where our second Bensham walk ends. Here you will be able to access local bus services.

Our fourth walk is around **Saltwell** and is approximately 2 miles.

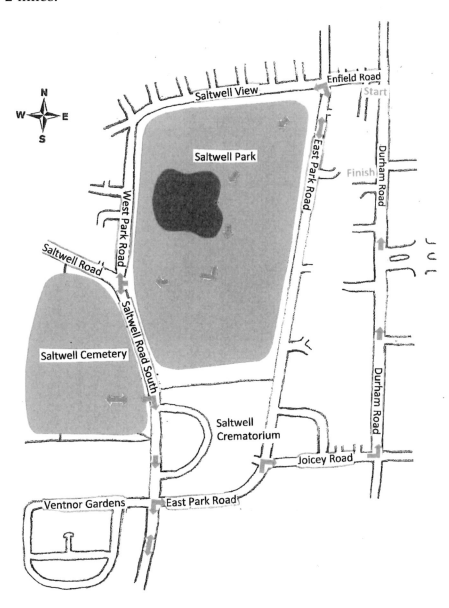

We start our walk at the corner of Durham Road and Enfield Road, notice in the stone wall a blocked up old carriage entrance to Enfield House.

Enfield House was a nineteen roomed house and stood at the top right hand corner of Enfield Road and Durham Road, roughly where William Wailes Walk is today. Thomas Neilson received planning approval to build a villa on

4 August 1865. One well-known occupier was the grocer Walter Willson. The house was later conveyed to Gateshead Corporation, and became a girls training college before Gateshead Technical College was built. The site is now Park View housing development.

From here walk down Enfield Road onto East Park Road. Turn left and walk along to the stairs leading up to Park View. Here you will see a stone plaque in the wall depicting the old Gateshead coat of arms. This plaque used to be above the doorway of the Gateshead College workshop buildings that stood near here.

We now retrace our steps along East Park Road to the main entrance of Saltwell Park which opened in 1876. Observe the goat heads on the outer two gate pillars, notice the one on the left, this is the only example where you will see the head in reverse.

Walk through the gates into Saltwell Park and down to the broad walk, note the wooden shelter to your left, one of two shelters built in 1882.

Take the footpath to your right down to the lake and pause before the play area. Look back over the grassed area towards the pavilion. Built in 1881 to provide refreshments, later renamed the Almond Pavilion after Mr G.E. Almond who donated the clock in 1903.

From here walk between the children's play areas, follow the path to the left then turn right into the Rose Garden. We now pass the Workers Memorial and cut through the garden and turn left then right before the foot bridge. A little further down turn left into Saltwell Dene. Make your way down through the dene, criss-crossing over the bridges. Hidden amongst the foliage you will come across the 2006 art work called 'Wriggle' by Colin Rose which represents rhythm patterns in nature. As you leave the dene you come across the old Salte Welle (*shown right*) restored in 1872 by William Wailes who owned the land that we know today as Saltwell Park.

At the base of the well is an old grate cover with the letters S P denoting Saltwell Park.

To the left of the well is one of the many park buildings, this is Dene Lodge which was at one time occupied by the park policeman.

We leave the park near West Park Road corner through the beautiful Art Nouveau style gates which were built by Gateshead firm Bainbridge & Crimson.

Turn right here and walk a little way round the corner where you will see the parish boundary stone of St Chad's on West Park Road. It now marks the point where the three present day parishes of St Chad's, St George's and St Helen's meet.

From here glance over West Park Road and admire Ferndene Lodge, behind which used to stand Ferndene House, which was built for Robert Stirling Newall in the early 1850s. In the grounds stood an observatory that housed the largest telescope of the time, and received many noted visitors. Note the blue plaque on the lodge to Robert Stirling Newall, commissioned by Gateshead Local History Society in April 2018.

Retrace your steps back to the park gates, and walk along Saltwell Road South, parallel with Saltwell Park until you come to a large brick building on your left. Here cross over the road to Saltwell Cemetery built in 1905 on land belonging to the late 16th century Saltwell Hall.

Walk through the gate and take the path straight ahead down between section G and F to the cross roads, on your left you will see an old stone wall which is all that remains of the former Hall.

We now retrace our steps up this path back onto Saltwell Road South via two large stone pillars which could have been an entrance to Saltwell Hall.

Opposite you can see the entrance to Saltwell Crematorium, this was originally the entrance to a house called Team Lodge, later renamed Endsleigh.

Now turn right, a little further long you will come to the old Nine Pins footpath (*shown right*) which was an old route to the Teams, now unfortunately a dead end.

In the early 1950s the small path off Saltwell Road next to the cemetery became the evening meeting place in the summer by a few pupils of the Gateshead Grammar School.

My friends and I used to meet there, although we had just been together at school. The estate next to it was just being built and so was the pub which became 'The Nine Pins' now 'Park View,' and why they have changed I have no idea!

Some of the girls came from the Whitehall Road area and I came from Earlswood Avenue, along Jessel Street and down Belle View Bank so I expect it was more or less a central point to meet. It was also quite private so we could congregate and discuss the rather dishy, mystery older boy who often joined us on his bicycle.

For some reason we never ventured down to the bottom of the path and to this day I still don't know what is there.

Shirley Brown

Opposite this you will see the exit for the crematorium which was the old entrance to South Dene Tower, a beautiful castellated building in red and white brick built by Mr W. Carr around 1851. South Dene Tower and land was sold to Gateshead Corporation by George Simonds' personal representatives on 1 February 1938, later  being demolished for the building of the crematorium.

From here we walk along past Park View public house, originally the Nine Pins which was built on the site of Saltwell Cottage. Carry on past the bus stop where you come to steps on your right that lead to Ventnor Gardens and Ventnor Crescent. Ventnor Gardens was built in the 1950s for workers of the Baltic Flour mill.

We now cross back over Saltwell Road South, and just to your right you can see a lovely cast iron pillar in the wall of Woodside House. Its original purpose is not clear. It may have been a gatepost or downpipe carrying rain water away from the house.

Passing  street sign you will see two modern houses in the dene on your right, this area is where Whinney House Dene joins Saltwell Dene. A little further along you will see some old railings which mark the boundary of the former Whinney House estate.

THE CROFT

Before we turn up East Park Road, known locally as dangerous hill, note the stone pillar on your right. As you continue up the road you will see more of these neat stone posts.

At the junction with Joicey Road you will see an entrance to Saltwell Park car park, this formed the back entrance to South Dene Tower (*shown below*).

Now walk up Joicey Road, just over half way up on your right you can see the former Joicey Road Open Air School now converted into business premises.

The school was opened in 1937 to provide education for 'physically handicapped and delicate' children.

Continue up Joicey Road, near the top on your left hand side you will see two truncated stone pillars with the words The Chesters.

Just before the top of Joicey Road, on your left, you will see a large stone pillar (*shown below*), which would have originally been the entrance to The Chesters, the home of Emerson Shephard the store proprietor and is now a nursing home. The original entrance can be seen circled on the 1939 map below.

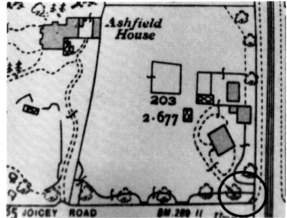

At the top of Joicey Road turn left along Durham Road, note the newly introduced cyclist/pedestrian sign in the footpath.

A little way along on the right hand side you will see Musgrave House, which was originally called Forres Villa. The house was built in 1854 for J.B. Falconer, a brown paper manufacturer. The house was later used as a school from 1919 until the 1990s when it closed and became apartments.

Now on your left hand side you will come to Heathfield House and Lodge. Heathfield House was built for Joseph Willis Swinburne in 1856 and is now residential apartments. The magnificent gateway is once again looking as impressive as it did when built.

Just past Heathfield Lodge is another entrance with two substantial stone pillars. Carry on north along Durham Road and on your left hand side you will come to the entrance pillars of The Drive, which have marked the entrance since around the beginning of the 20th century.

To the right there is a blue plaque to Katherine Githa Sowerby, the daughter of John George Sowerby the glass manufacturer. She was a playwright and children's author and lived at Ravenshill situated at the bottom of The Drive.

We now carry on along Durham Road until you come to a high stone wall behind which is North Dene. Note the letters and number denoting the position of a fire hydrant, during war years the figures would have been painted black. Look out for more random letters as you walk along.

North Dene, an impressive stone building with large gardens, was built in 1853 for Richard Wellington Hodgson. In later years the house was used as part of Gateshead Grammar School, and then part of Gateshead College, now being converted into apartments.

Carry on past the high stone wall, where we come to this old exit sign, once the road way out of the college car park.

This is where our Saltwell walk ends.

Our fifth walk is around **Shipcote** and is approximately 1.5 miles.

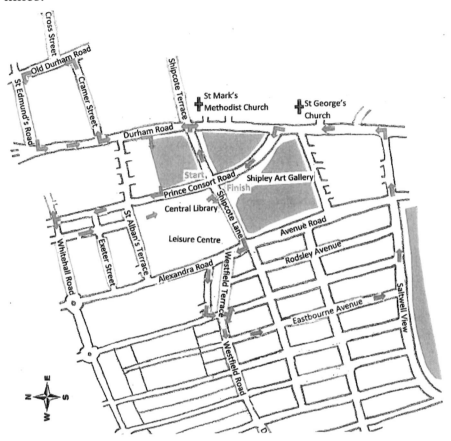

We start our walk at the junction of Shipcote Lane and Prince Consort Road beside the stone boundary wall of the little park. This area was once the grounds of South Close Villa which stood in the far north corner of the park.

> The little park next to the garage would have come about when the big house South Close Villa which was on that site until 1950 was demolished. Two spinster ladies left it to the council for poor ladies of the parish to be housed in it. My dad was caretaker until 1950. Gateshead council pulled the house down and made it into a park. The nursery was at the back of the house facing onto Prince Consort Road.
>
> *Moira Inness*

Walk down Shipcote Lane to Durham Road, notice the street sign of Balmoral Terrace on the opposite side of the road. Another interesting street sign is Kensington Terrace just past St Mark's Church on the corner of Chandos Street and Durham Road.

At the traffic lights cross over Durham Road, turn left and walk along to Cramer Street, and turn right. On reaching Old Durham Road turn right and walk over the crossing. Walk down to Cross Street and turn right, further along you will see the old ornate Cross Hotel.

From here retrace your steps to Old Durham Road and turn right note the street sign for St Edmund's Place walk down past

the row of houses and observe the second street sign of St Edmund's Place. We now pass St Edmund's cemetery on your right. Look for the obelisk erected by the then Rector of Gateshead John Collinson to commemorate the 222 victims who died of cholera between December 1831 and November 1832. Note the inscription 'In the midst of life we are in death' and 'Watch therefore for ye know not what hour your Lord doth come'. A little further down you will see the lovely drinking fountain.

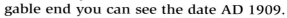

Next observe the old cemetery gateway now blocked up. Passing the Rectory you will see a stone panel in the wall to the King James Hospital that formerly stood on this site. On the gable end you can see the date AD 1909.

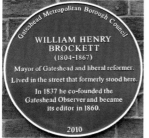

Next we come to a blue plaque to William Henry Brockett, co-founder of the Gateshead Observer who lived in the street that formerly stood here.

From here a little further down on your right is the lovely

Carefully cross the road and walk to the bottom of Old Durham Road, look up at the end house to see the two street signs.

We now head up Old Durham Road, note the stone plaque in the wall of the end house.

Now carry on to St Edmund's Road, turn right and walk to Durham Road. Turn right to the crossing and cross over Durham Road then turn left. As you walk along observe the white brick houses to the opposite side of the road. Just before the road on your right look at the street sign of Noble Terrace. Continue along Durham Road, alongside the low wall just past the opening into the park observe the cast iron G.P.O. cable junction marker (*shown below*).

Now walk through the park towards Prince Consort Road, where you can see a stone pillar in the wall to your right denoting an old entrance of South Close Villa.

We now turn right along Prince Consort Road noting the many impressive old storm porches on the houses on both sides of the road. At Whitehall Road turn right then walk a short distance to the lane on your right.

Here on the gable end you will see an old advertisement painted directly onto the wall. This has a black background with a white and yellow border. The original advertisement in white says IDEAL BAKERY FOR DELICIOUS CAKES AND PASTRIES, and superimposed in yellow is IDEAL BAKERY PHONE 71779.

From here we take a few steps back to Prince Consort Road and take the crossing to Whitehall Road, notice the stone and brick adornments on the houses to the right. Then turn left through the back lane to Exeter Street noting the street sign on the first house on the right.

Continue through the lane, look out for the round cover in the road with WC on. At the end turn left, on the street corner you will see the sign for St Alban's Terrace, cross over and head towards Gateshead Central Library.

Look at the building on your right which opened as the Borough Treasurers Department in 1954. The building had a circular single-storey ratings hall adjacent to a two-storey office block, later increased to three storeys in 1972-74. After the opening of the Civic Centre in 1987 it became a training centre and Social Services offices until around 2014 and is currently unoccupied.

If the library is open walk through the side entrance and into the lending library, on the wall to your left is the plaque marking the opening ceremony on 31 March 1926. The Library's initial design by architect Arthur Stockwell was too costly. Stockwell died and another architect David Ditchburn was appointed and a reduced design was accepted in 1925/26. The building was extended in the 1970s and again in 2011.

Just before the exit you will pass on your left a 'dumb waiter' originally used to transport books up and down from 'the stack' on the level below.

Now walk through the foyer area of the original entrance, look up and see the lovely original glass dome and moulded architrave ceiling, which have now been complemented by the modern decorative glass wall panels leading to the study rooms on either side.

Leaving from the library's main entrance turn right and right again down Shipcote Lane, the area to your right was the site of Shipcote House and farm. The building further along on your right, now incorporated into Gateshead Leisure Centre, is Shipcote Baths. The Leisure Centre was opened on 6 November 1981 by Her Majesty the Queen.

From here we take the path on your right round to the back of the building, in the brick wall you will see the foundation stone laid on 24 July 1939.

From the age of twelve (1960) my mam allowed me and a group of mates to go to Shipcote Baths by ourselves. We were given our bus fares but always spent the return fare on a 'penny dip' (half a bun dipped in gravy) from the shop on Alexandra Road, then walked home to Felling.

Bob Dixon

Now on Alexandra Road cross over to the Corporation Club. This was originally Westfield Hall and the first home of the Progressive Players founded by members of the Independent Labour Party in 1920. The group later moved to the Little Theatre on Saltwell View which we will see later on the walk.

We now walk down the back lane between the club and the houses. Along the small lane on your right is an old building currently a builder's yard which was built in 1932 as a 'Pop' (soft drinks) factory. The pop was manufactured on the upper floor and was lowered from a large hatch to the carts below. Note the shiny red bricks that clad the walls of the ground floor which was originally the stables. Also note the other old buildings as you walk along the back lane onto Coatsworth Road.

Don't miss the 'bumper' at ground level on your right as you emerge from the lane, put in place to prevent carts being damaged as they turned into the lane.

From here turn left and left again onto Westfield Terrace, on your left you can now see an old chapel built in 1932. The chapel has two interesting foundation stones, each with a Durham connection. One was laid by Henry Shaw Harrison, an Old Dunelmian (student of Durham School) who was head of Harrison and Harrison, the famous organ builders of Durham.

The second was laid by Canon Richard Dutton Budworth M.A. who was headmaster of Durham School from 1907 to 1932 and an England international rugby player in his time.

From here turn round towards Coatsworth Road junction, look at the view down towards St Chad's Church and beyond.

Walk down Westfield Road to the corner of Eastbourne Avenue. On your left is the Azure Blue public house, infamous for the murder of the Tyneside publican George Gill (Vivian) in 1994.

We now turn left and walk along Eastbourne Avenue passing the old co-operative store on your right. Also note some of the end of terrace ground floor buildings which were at one time shops, most now converted into houses.

At the end of Eastbourne Avenue turn left onto Saltwell View, an impressive terrace of houses. As you reach the Little Theatre note the metal balustrades above the windows of these houses.

The Little Theatre was built during the Second World War thanks to the generosity of sisters Ruth, Sylvia and Madelaine Hope Dodds. It is believed that the theatre was the only one built in Britain during the war. The first performance was 'A Midsummer Night's Dream' on Wednesday 13 October 1943.

Now walk up Enfield Road, on your left is one of the few remaining cobbled lanes left in Gateshead, imagine a horse and cart passing through. At the top of Enfield Road turn right and take the crossing over Durham Road to the Victorian row of houses with the street name Milne Terrace on the end of the wall.

We now turn left along Durham Road, to your right you will come to the old entrance of Lindum House. 'Lindum' was the original Roman name for the town of Lincoln. Lindum House was built for Thomas Wright and was known as the 'House with a Handle' due to the ornamental metal-work that joined the two small chimney stacks on the roof. The house is currently being renovated back to a private residence. At the boundary between Lindum House and the residential home to its left, look up to see the remains of a large signpost, a reminder of the Springfield Hotel which once stood on this site.

Continue along Durham Road, at the junction with Dryden Road you will see the former Shipcote Hall Cinema which opened on 10 December 1911, later named the Shipcote Picture Hall which closed on 16 April 1960. The building later became

a Hardy's furniture store and is now a health club and snooker hall. Cross back over Durham Road and continue towards the Cenotaph, look out for the lovely mosaic tiled shop entrance showing 'Maynards Ltd', at one-time a sweet shop.

Now to your left is Edendale Terrace, look up to see the 221B sign. Did Sherlock Holmes live here?

Our walk now takes us to the junction of Durham Road and Prince Consort Road passing the site of the old Grammar School built in 1883. The building was

demolished in 1963 and a new school built which was re-named in 1967 as Saltwell Senior High School, a co-educational comprehensive school which lasted until the 1990s when it was closed and partially demolished after a fire.

From here on the opposite side of the road is St George's Church which has one of the best organs in the North East. It is a Father Willis, named after the founder of the company of organ builders Henry Willis and is maintained by Harrison's of Durham. Remember Henry Shaw Harrison mentioned earlier in the walk.

Now in front of you is the Cenotaph. The Cenotaph is a grade II listed monument made of sandstone with a bronze door, designed by architect J.W. Spink of Kingston-on-Thames and was unveiled on 14 May 1922. The chamber originally housed the Roll of Honour of Gateshead men who were killed in the Great War which is now kept at Gateshead Central Library.

We now walk along Prince Consort Road passing on your left a stone pillar with the imprint of the word 'IN' on it. This tall gatepost at one time marked the access road curving up to the Shipley Art Gallery, as can be seen in this postcard below.

Shipley Art Gallery, Gateshead.

It is hard to imagine it now as Prince Consort Road has been widened and a footpath added to the front of the gallery. In the art gallery grounds you can see the memorial to James Renforth the famous rower who died in Canada in 1871. The art gallery was opened in 1917 having been funded by the wealthy local solicitor and art collector, Joseph Ainsley Davidson Shipley. From outside the gallery look towards the little park and a Second World War memorial in the stone wall. This little park was once the grounds of St Edmund's Vicarage.

We now pass what remains of the 'OUT' pillar as we come to the former Education Offices building built by Gateshead School Board in 1897. This is where our Shipcote walk ends.

We hope you have enjoyed the five walks in this book. There will be two further books in our series Uncovering Gateshead.